From the Book of Remembrance

From the Book of Remembrance

poems and paintings

Karla Van Vliet

Shanti Arts Publishing
Brunswick, Maine

FROM THE BOOK OF REMEMBRANCE

Copyright © 2015 Karla Van Vliet

All Rights Reserved
No part of this book may be used or reproduced
in any manner whatsoever without the
written permission of the publisher.

Published by Shanti Arts Publishing
Cover and interior design by Shanti Arts Designs
Cover image: *Meeting at the Horizon*

Shanti Arts LLC
193 Hillside Road, Brunswick, Maine 04011
shantiarts.com

Printed in the United States of America

First edition
10 9 8 7 6 5 4 3 2 1

ISBN: 978-1-941830-23-9 (softcover)
ISBN: 978-1-941830-24-6 (digital)

Library of Congress Control Number: 2015948359

Publisher's Cataloging-In-Publication Data:
available upon request

To all who dare follow
their hearts to the Beloved.

Contents

Paintings

Hold me in this darkest of places
where I cannot see
but know only by feel
this body which is the land of me.

Beloved
(of earth)

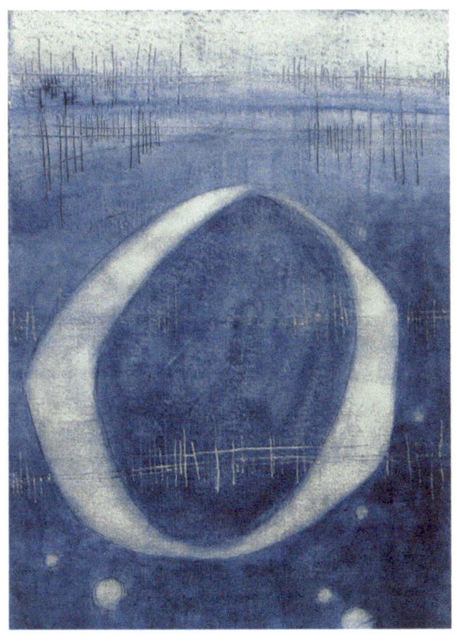

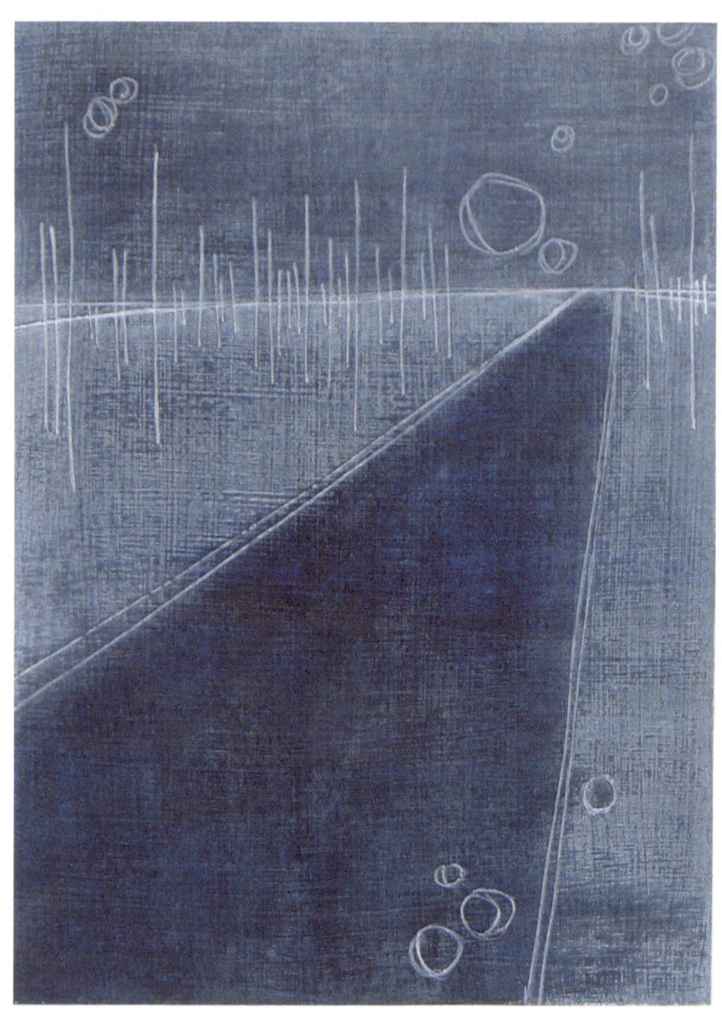

Post: From My Kitchen

•

It is dinner time and I am cooking in my kitchen. I am imagining you come up behind me. I think to say the moon is but a sliver and holds the sky like your hand on my hip. Of course you do not hear me, you at your own stove two states away. I think, the sand hill cranes have come back again, four summers now. I think of their wings held to the shape of a crescent. I think, if I were a crane I would leave the burgers to burn. I would fly east toward your long wooden table, my wings like two napkins flapping. The sound they'd make like smacking lips.

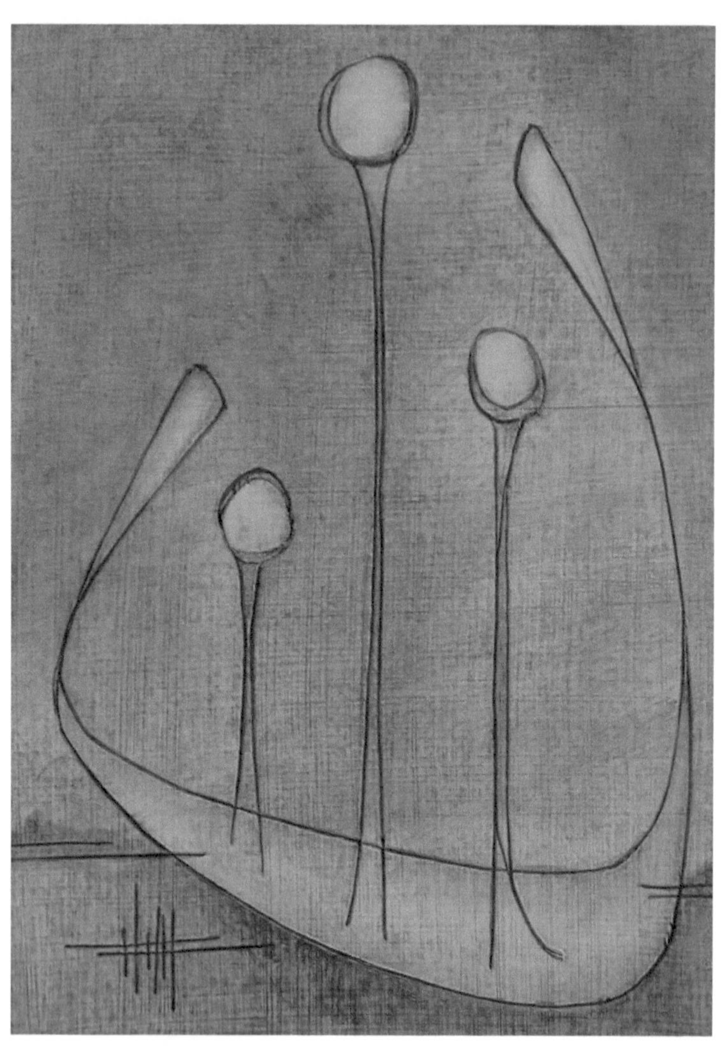

Post: From the Verge of Sleep

•

The room is cool; the night's wet air filling the darkness. My head rests on your shoulder and I am on the verge of sleep. It has been the span of the waxing moon and our awkwardness, like a courting. Your easy scent covers me like a warm quilt and I know I will sleep deeply, my body next to yours. I think, this is what feeling safe is, this is me setting down the leaded-shield of my vigilance. I think, this is like the power of the river: a clear strong flowing. You are whispering the Lord's Prayer above me and your voice, let loose in the wind, sails, sails, white petals across the lawn.

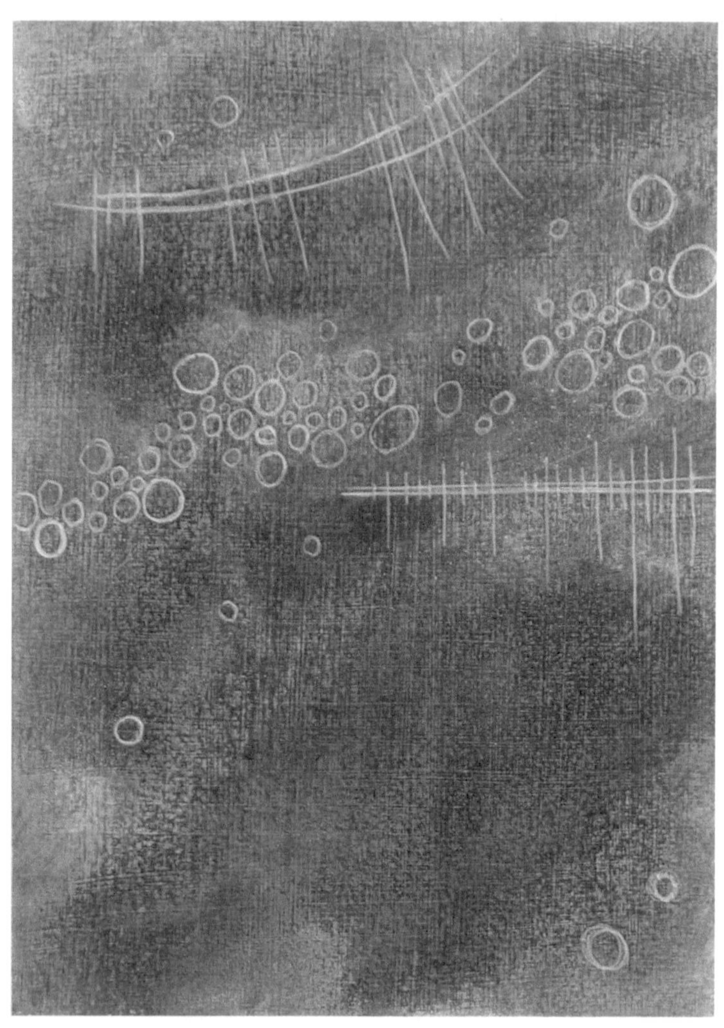

Post: From the Border of Bidding You Farewell

•

Above, a lone dark bird glides over. I stand in the driveway waving, even now after you are no longer visible. I know you will stop down the road at The Big Wheel, pump your gas, pick up a snack. And then you will wind your way up along the river into the mountains. The afternoon is a stretch of long hours. I stand and watch the clouds build to the north. A car drives by. I turn and enter the house. Here, the place your body just was, where I knew the hungry wet pleasure of your love, where my hands spoke our private language across the leisure of your skin, where your hands answered, this place, is empty of you. It is a desolate country.

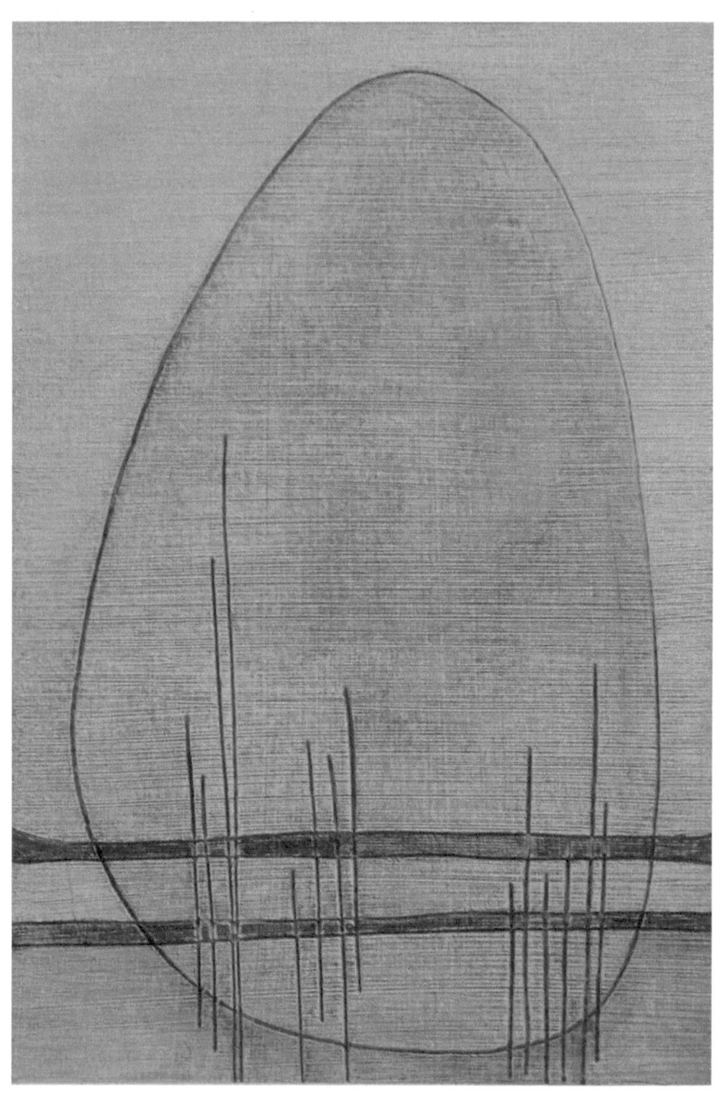

Post: From the Curved Edge of Your Daughter's Body

•

Light filtering dream from memory; your bed is like a great field petaled white. The trunk and limbs of me, like an apple tree. I woke early and can smell the coffee you brew downstairs, hear the making of food. I imagine how you will come to me bearing coffee and toast, the way my grandfather brought my grandmother her breakfast in bed. Here, your daughter lies in the shelter of my body, curled in upon herself. Like the calf I found in the meadow those many years ago, quiet and waiting, unsure if I am the enemy. Or the haven she had sought.

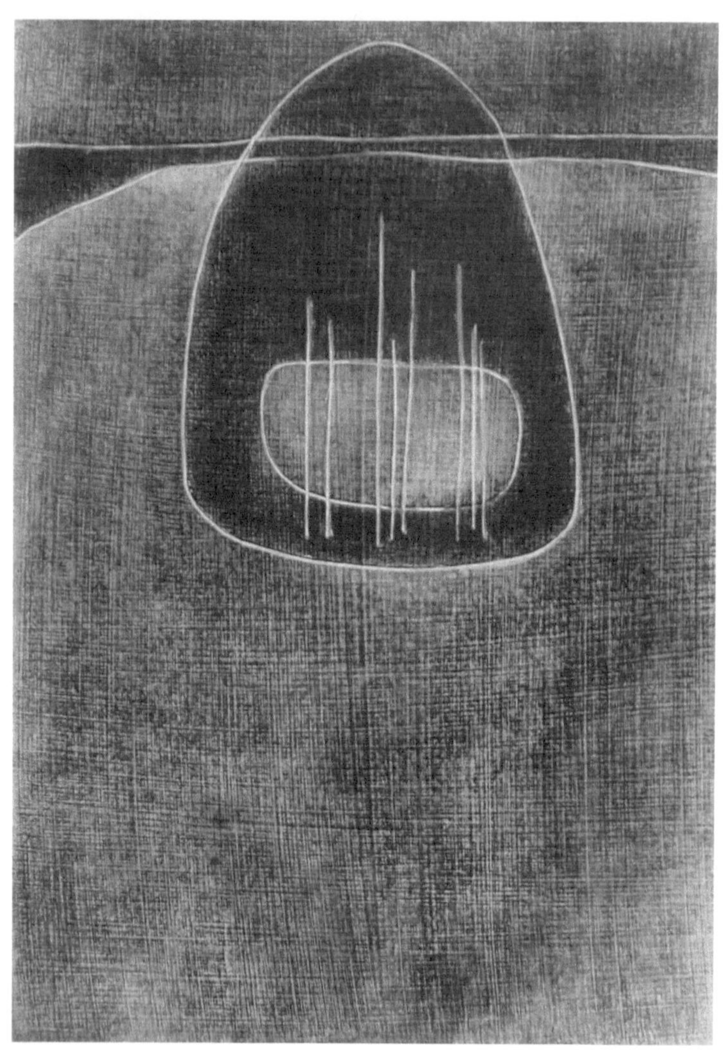

Post: From Scarborough Beach

•

I'm thinking, the way I keep falling in love with you is like these waves. There are easy swells, which lift me off my feet and waves that crest against my chest. We swim in these, laze about or whoop and holler. This is like our day-to-day love. But then there is the wave that comes every so often, the big one, I see it coming, feel it, as the water pulls at my legs, surges up, so high, way over my head, and I think, oh shit, how am I going to survive this. The way my breath catches and fear tastes in my mouth. I think, I will be consumed here. I think, I want nothing more than to be consumed here. Because now I am not in my skin, not contained. I am trying to find my element. Sitting on the blanket I watch you with the kids down by the shore. It can be that simple. I look at you.

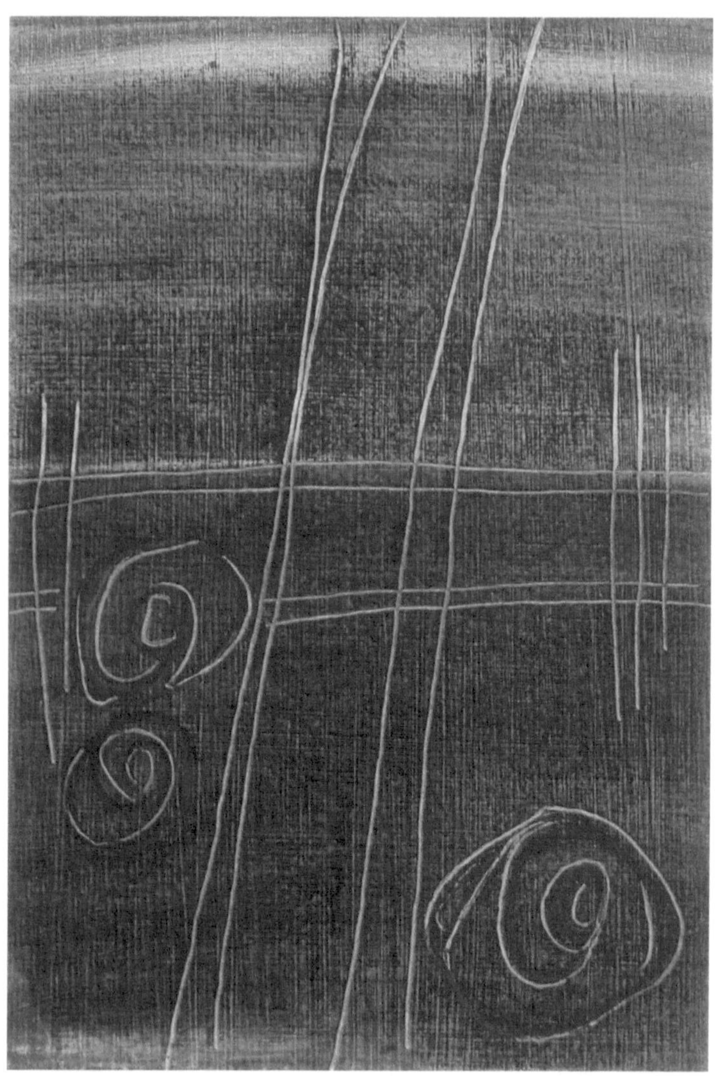

Post: From Beneath Petaled Branches

•

The tree has blossomed. I am lying on the cool wet grass beneath the apple. From here the world is all blue and brown and white light. In my dream the orchard orioles in the branches above drape my body, petal by petal, the pattern of my wedding dress. Their burnt orange bodies nest in my hair and I rise to stand before you a wild creature. In my dream you recite the words given you by the white stallion grazing in the field beyond. I open my mouth and my oath lifts from my tongue in blue butterflies. I am lying on the cool wet grass. You my darling, my beloved, are driving towards me, by now you'll be winding over Bethel Mountain Road, soon you will pull in the drive. It will take the evening to recognize you.

Beloved
(of heaven)

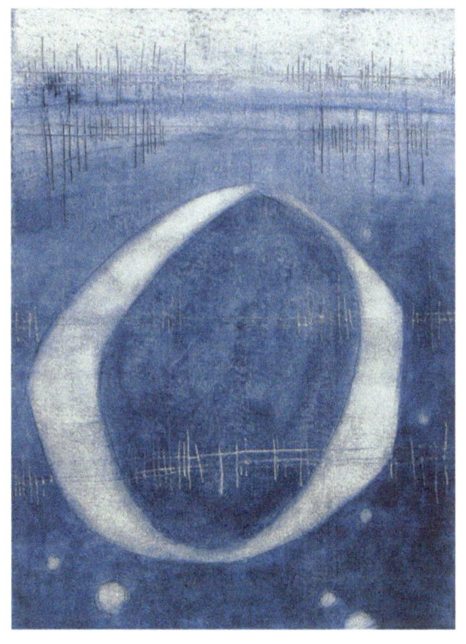

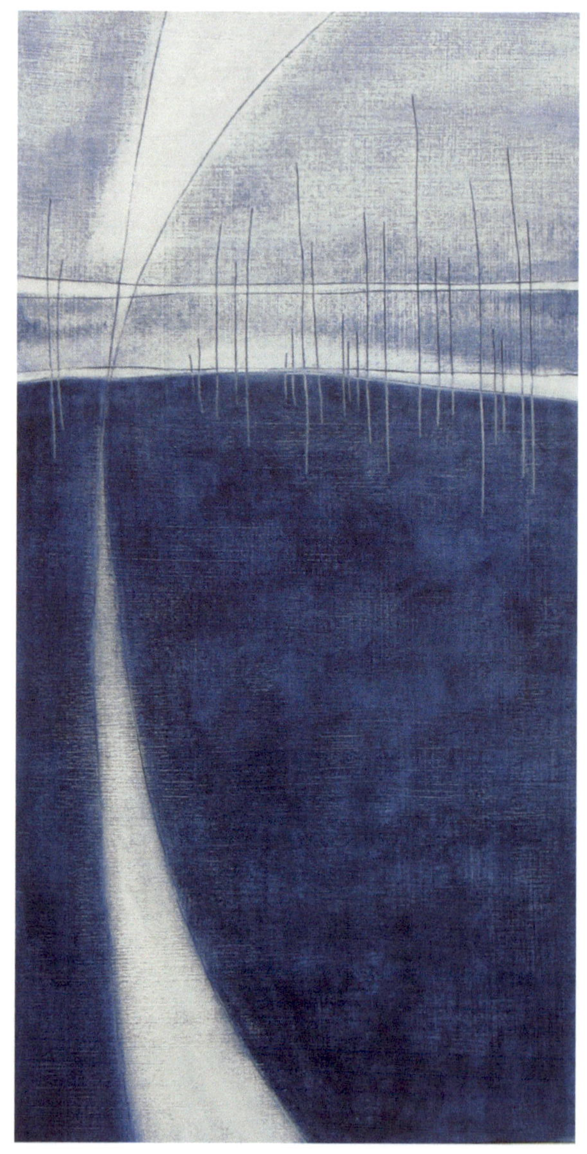

Post: From the Book of Remembrance (Burning)

•

Here the trees are tall and close. Somewhere far off a crow caws in urgent sharpness, above the leaves shuffle. There is a kind of loneliness here. As a child I built a shrine to you in a wood like this. It was out behind our house in Lincoln. I was, what, seven or eight? The shrine made of the arched roots of a tree. I hid matches there. And even though I knew kids weren't suppose to play with matches I lit one each evening as a kind of vespers. A token of flame to show for the rage of burning inside my young heart, I who needed you in a forest fire of longing, my gesture, an asking, a prayer, my turning to ash. Girl who was me, what were you made of? A tumble of soot and bone.

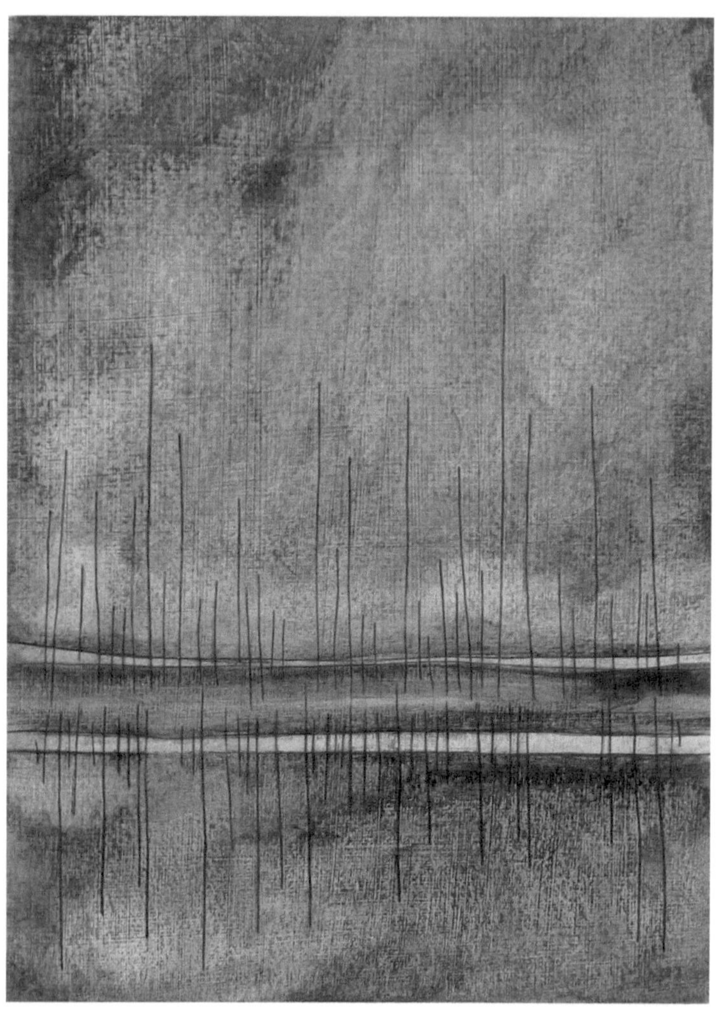

Post: From the Book of Remembrance (Waiting For You)

•

I waited for you but you did not come. In their vase, the flowers dried to paper thin then sifted dust across the table. The sky suffered a hundred migrations. My breath held hot and empty. For sure you knew my anguish. How could you not hear the pleading in my songs, those little prayers I sent up to you from the tangle of my bed? You did not come. You did not come, even on my knees. How could I survive? Outside the world turned to sand and drifted into every shoe and eye. Where were you? I carried faith like a torch of fury.

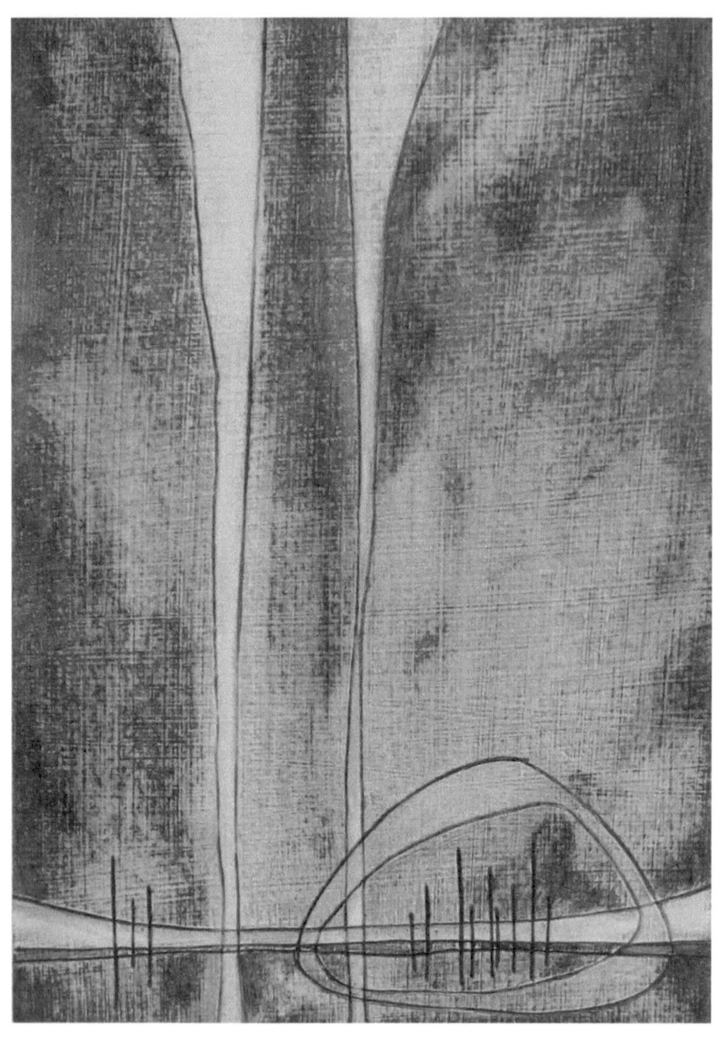

Post: From the Book of Remembrance (Come Soon)

•

Today I listened for you. I thought maybe you would come, like Dad, down the driveway, the springs on the GMC rasping for every dip and pot-hole. And something in my heart would leap for the sound of it. Yet I heard nothing just the breeze in the tree tops, the buzzing of insects. I thought, well then. And then, maybe you would come, in say, some kind of weather phenomena; a storm, maybe heavy winds or rains or a tornado. I watched out the window but saw only the dip and dive of the blue-jay. Then I thought, well maybe you would come in a swarm of dragonflies over the field or some fierce animal would show up, cross my path, say, a catamount, even though the rangers say they don't exist here anymore. That would be kind of perfect because I don't know if you exist anymore either. I got into the car and drove for miles on the back roads waiting for the sign but only saw the Johnson's black lab and I have to say I don't like labs. You know some days I'm left wondering. Sending off this note to you: come soon.

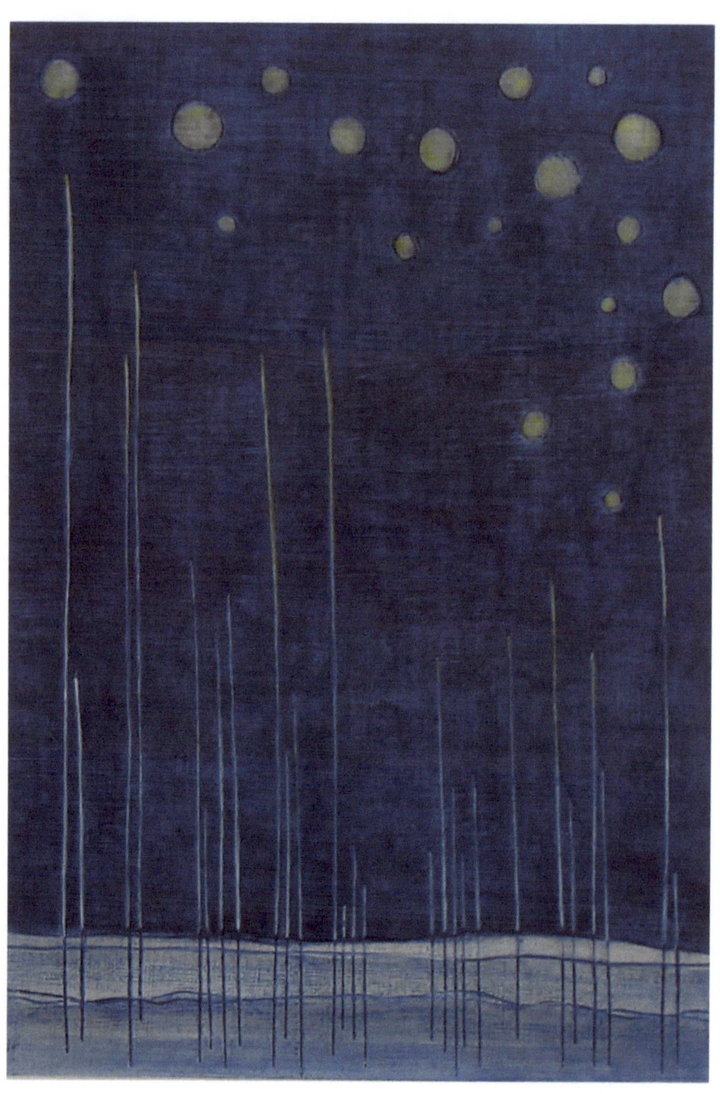

Post: From the Book of Remembrance (Darkness)

•

I am in a mood. Dark and winged and blackening the sky like roosting crows swarming the hillside. I pull the curtains against you, against even the birds settling in the branches. I want none of it. Not your light, not the absolved blue, not even the rustled agitation in the thicket. It is absolute, such despair. I am on the floor. There is a theory in physics that darkness is light standing still and surely this is darkness. I could stay here. Despondency, a wept river. Brine to irrigate the fields of me. And then. What intervention to quicken the darkness? Zephyr or breath, lifting the blinds.

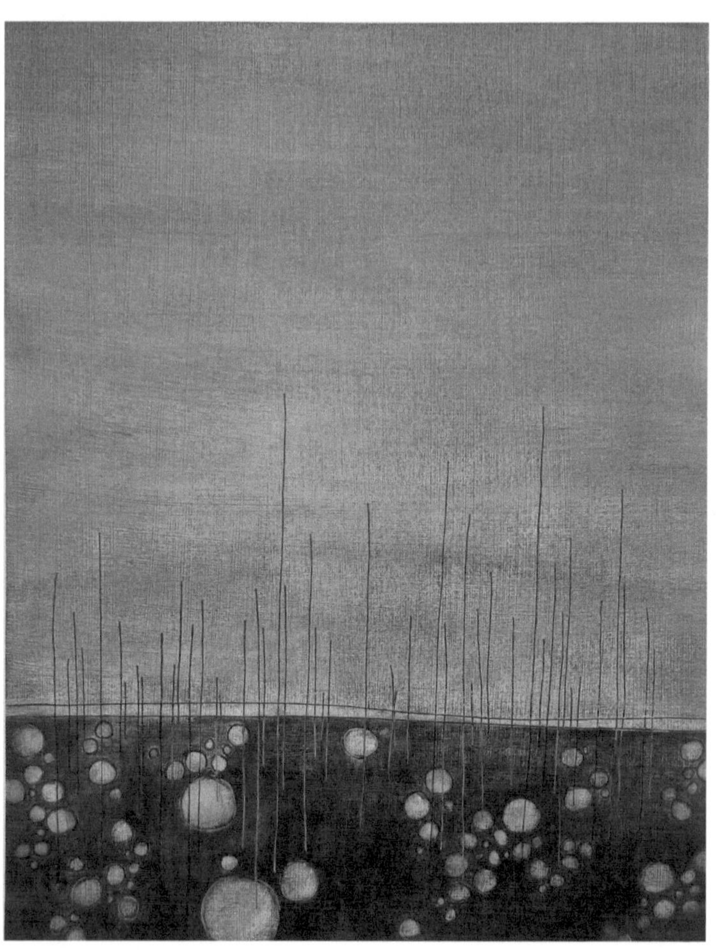

Post: From the Book of Remembrance (The Depths)

•

It is like this, I have not wanted to feel the depths of my love for you for as deep as my love so is my grief, having lost you. And I am dying of grief; I am a wild storm of grief. Do not tell.

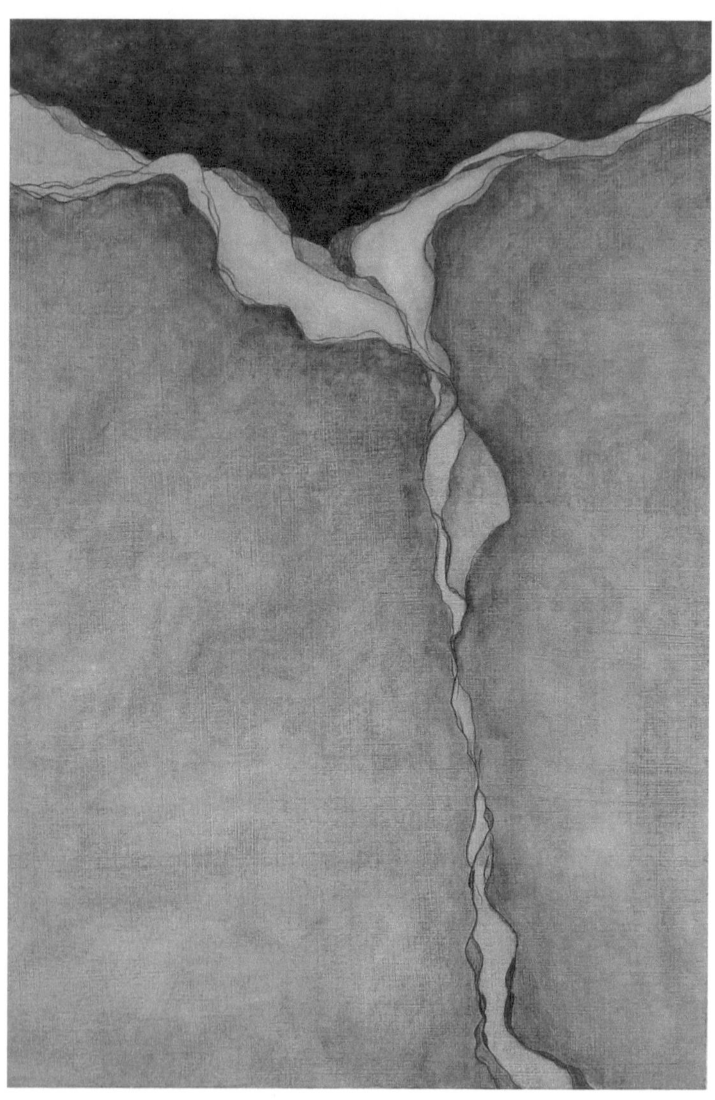

Post: From the Book of Remembrance (Caked In Salt)

•

How, when I am a lost traveler, when I am washed up on this shore caked in tear salt, how, under this burden of sorrow, can I love you? I swear, my devotion is a knife, damn you, damn you, my words all blood and spit. I feel like that bobcat I saw in Connecticut, caged and pacing, under its snarl the slit memory of wildness, utter and languished, the saddest thing.

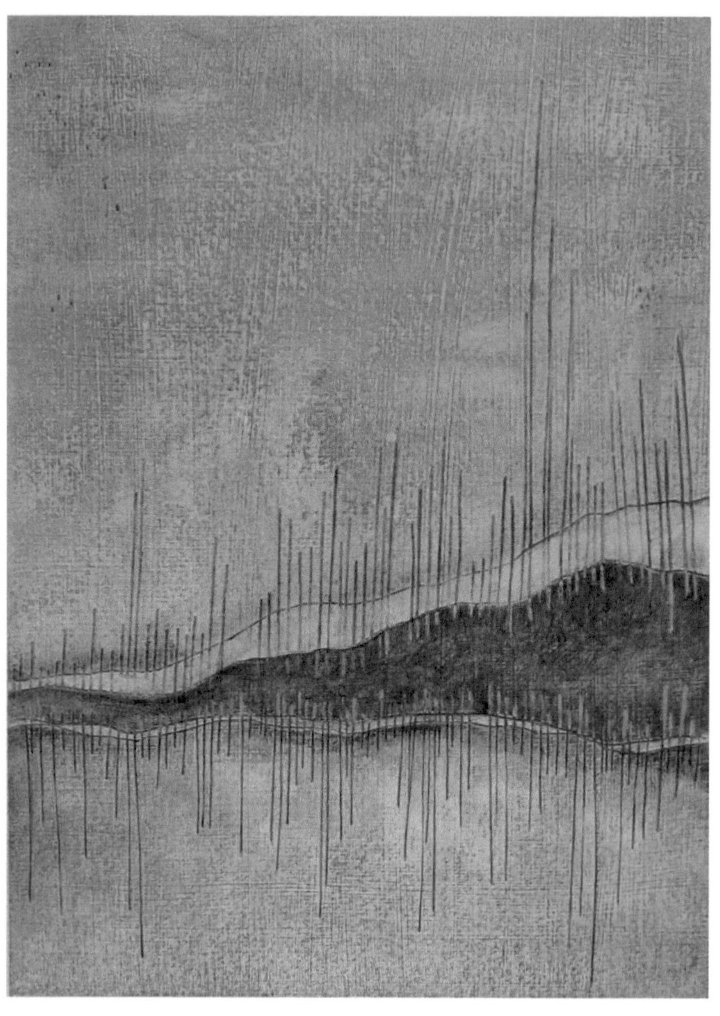

Post: From the Book of Remembrance (Perhaps It's Easier)

•

Perhaps it's easier to imagine you do not exist. At least then I could rip this terrible need up by the roots and toss it aside. I could say things like: *A god, you're nuts have you seen the state of the world?* I could say: *Let's fuck on this trashy old mattress, what's there to lose?* I could say: *Hand me the roach I had a shitty day.* I mean there have been days I thought, oh, to be the guy pumping gas, why can't I work at the seven/eleven. But who am I kidding; to untangle you from my body undoes me; chalice of my heart, like the tulip's flower, rising from the dark unknown.

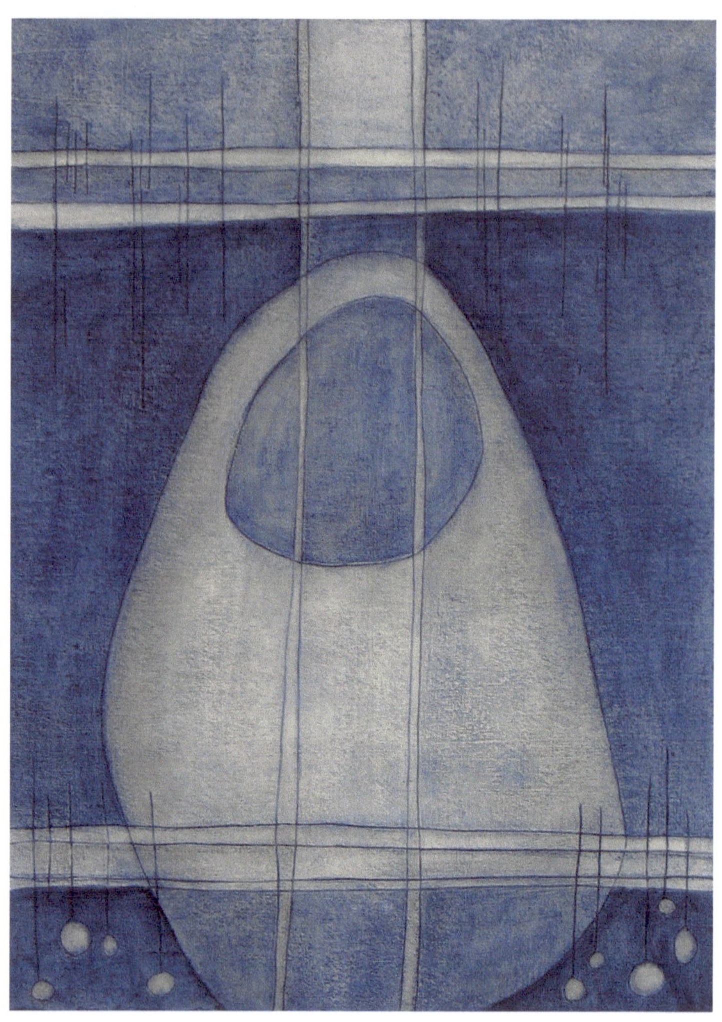

Post: From the Book of Remembrance (The Skinny)

•

Okay, God, this is the skinny: I have missed you like mad and not having you in my life is the worst heartache. I mean I love you like a crazy dog. And I know it's always me walking away; it hurts to love you so intensely. My every breath cuts and your love coursing through my body, hurts a little too. And when I breathe I am just so awake and every hurt I've ever felt comes back. But you are there holding me in my pain and there is nothing like being loved so tenderly. Which is why sometimes it's hard to accept and I walk away but I don't want to walk away anymore I want to stay, even though. I want your arms holding me like the night sky, like a rain, like the mountain stream, holding me until I cry out every wound, until I'm exhausted. Until I am emptied and there is room for something else.

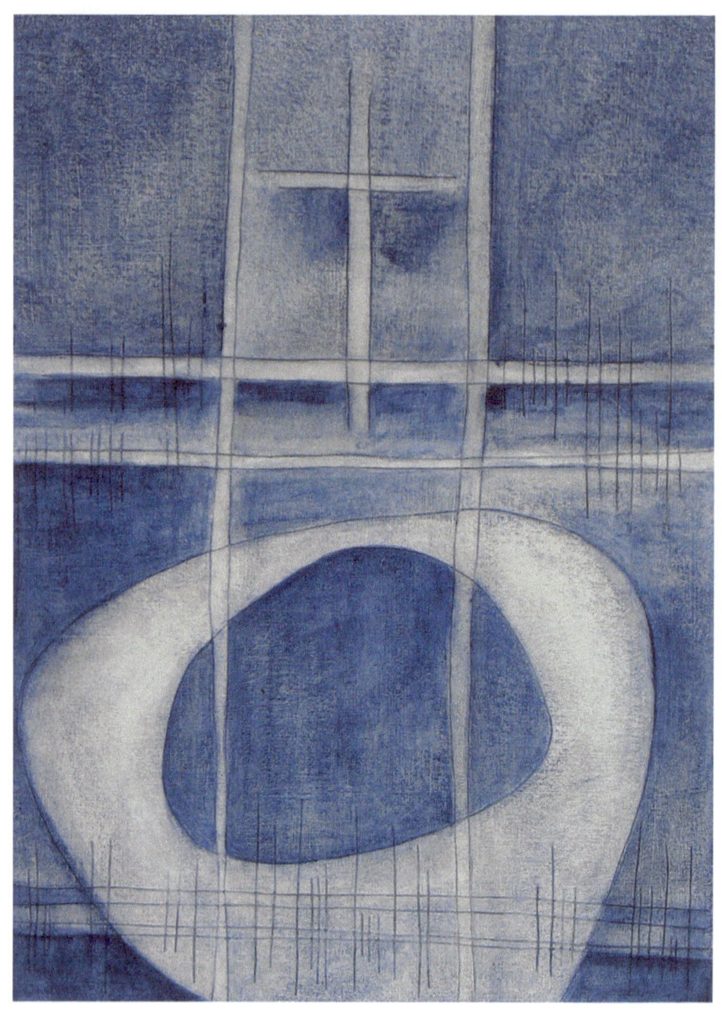

Post: From the Book of Remembrance (Your Breath)

•

I am standing at the window, it is dawn and light in the east is held close to the mountain. In the juniper tree, a flicker of red. And now I see the cardinal; its body like blood against the snow. I am that sorrow. God, without your breath, the storm of your breath stirring the despair of my living—if I am born of your body, let some winds of you still reside here. For I need a tempest of you to lay close, to lay me down. To awaken me. Look now, the bird has taken flight.

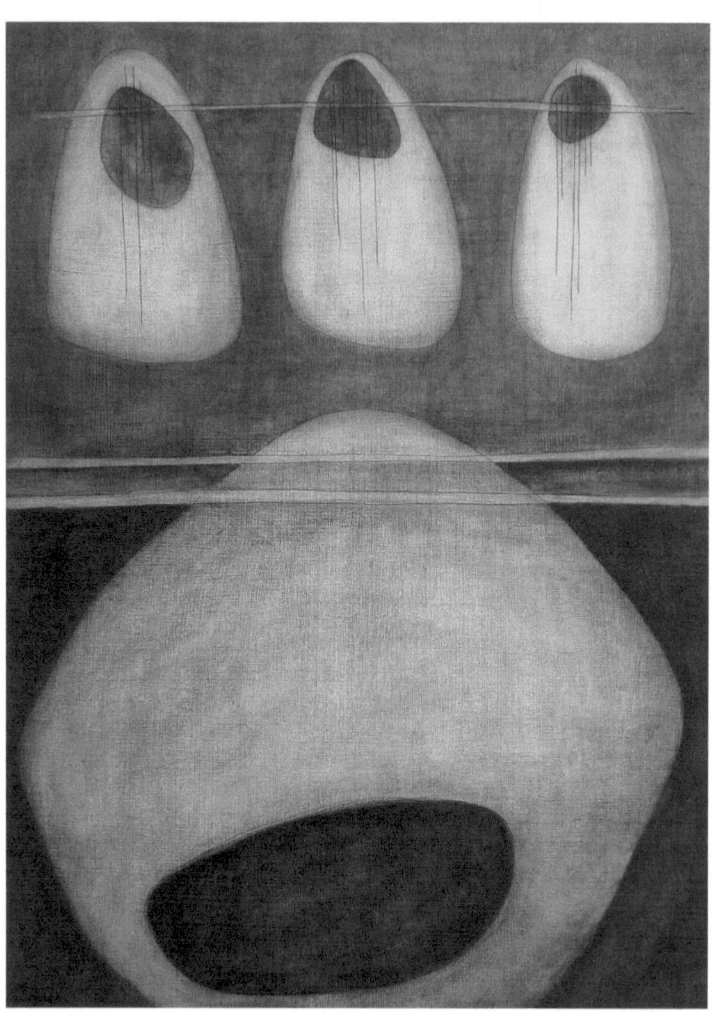

Post: From the Book of Remembrance (Storm's Brink)

•

The trees are dusk lit and rustle in the expectant storm. Birds fly low across the lawn their shadows rising and falling along the grass like stitches. I stand at the door, watch the clouds, gathered over the lake, roll across the valley. The sutures of trepidation cinch the air. At first I hear just a rumble, a far off train or a truck coming down the road, or fireworks out at Basin Harbor. But then, as if insisting itself the air splits. Ripping echoes off the mountain at my back. This is how it feels to love you, the sharp edge of need cutting the air, a fierce slitting. I have written a thousand love poems to you but never have I let you this close. I am standing in the whipping wind.

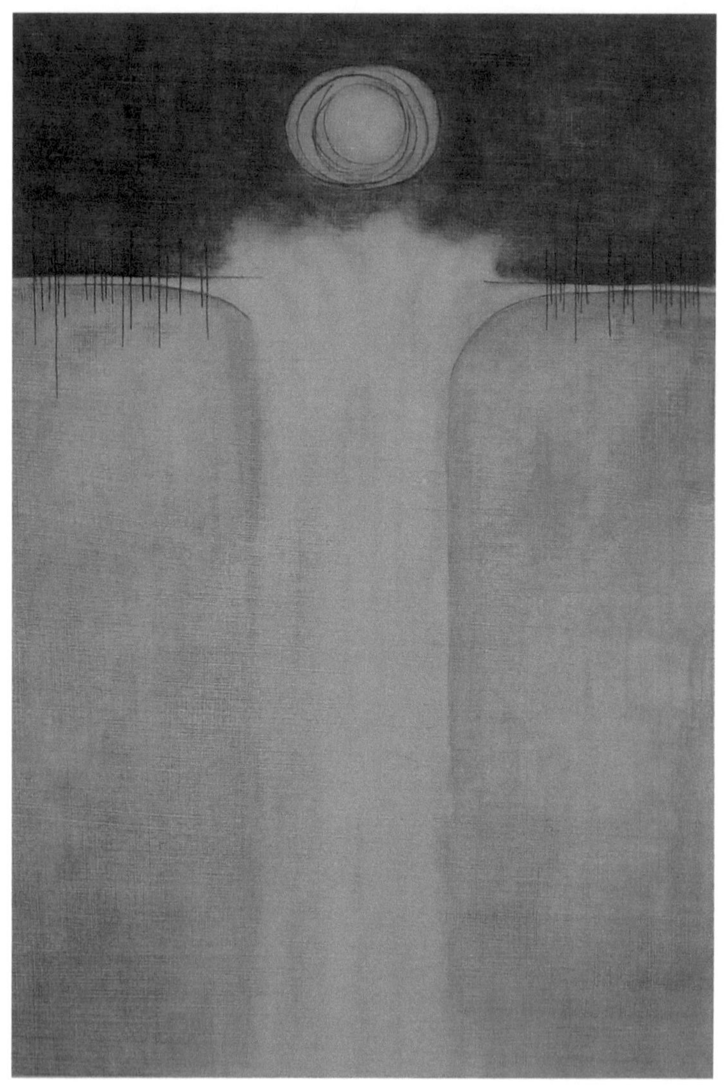

Post: From the Book of Remembrance (Wings)

•

In the night outside a torrent of rain has let loose. The air shifts. I shift and ache a little and think of you. The downpour sounds like the slapping of wings, a hundred snow geese taking flight. That's how I've been feeling recently, like a throng of birds breaking into a storm beat sky, my body aching with the tight turn of furious abandon. O let it pour, let it pour, let it pour.

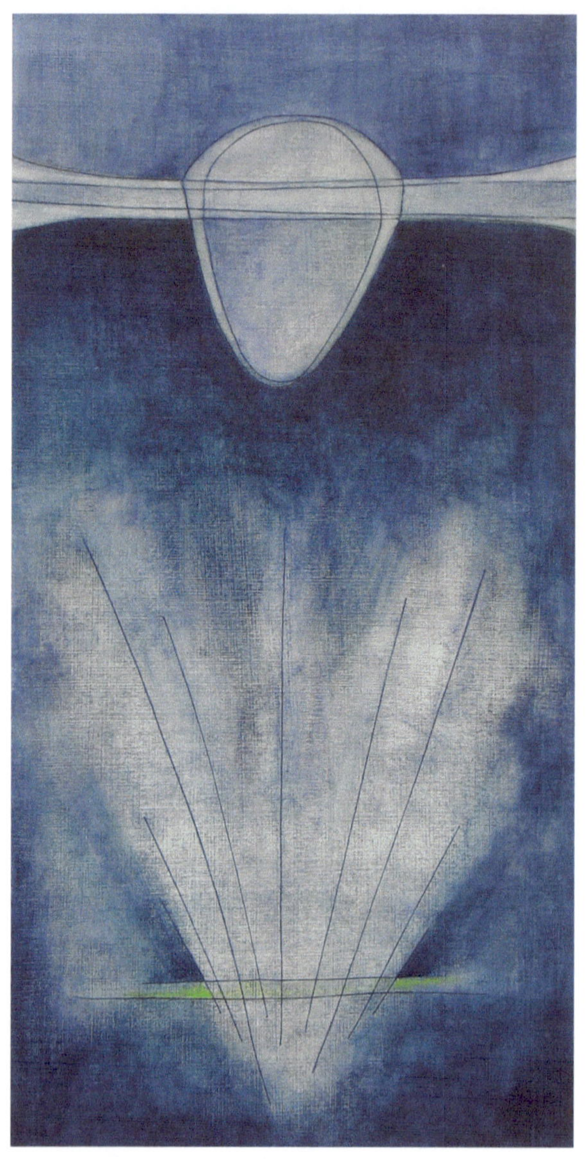

Post: From the Book of Remembrance (Let Loose)

•

It's still, here in quiet waking after the storm. Bird song surprises the air with its stripped honesty. And me, I am startled. Instinctively the cardinal calls and calls for his beloved, the browned body fidgeting the wild rose bush. And a stirring in me, so old, loosens and lets go, like breath, like some long held grief, the bird from the bush. It's said one must weep, one must lay out their sorrows, let those birds fill the sky, and today I just might believe what they say. The sun is breaking through the eastern clouds and I am flying.

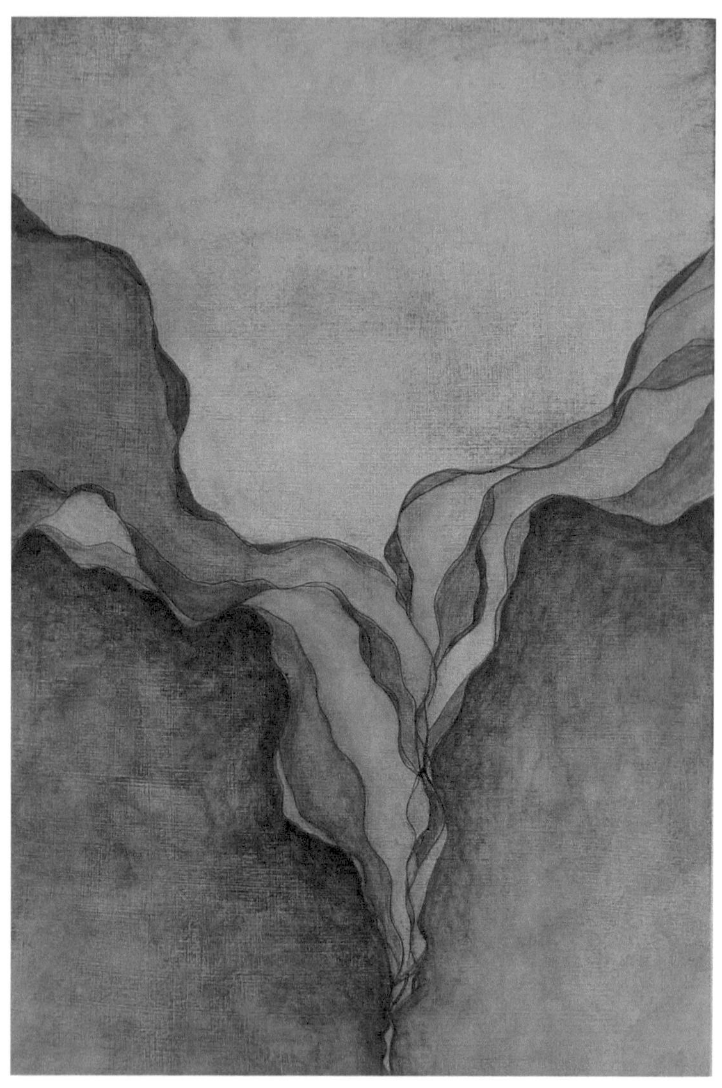

Post: From the Book of Remembrance (Dirt)

•

It is spring, at last it is spring. This winter so damn long, the snow piled up foot by foot. But I am done with all that, done. Done with the cold, the hibernation. Today the wet of spring rain is seeping into the damp earth and smells of all things awakening. I am setting the new bulbs, root side down, my hands covered in rich wet dirt, I am placing you on my tongue, I am eating the dirt which is you. I am putting you back inside of me I am returning you to me I am filling my self with you I am making my body of you. I take breath and speak with the dirt of you in my mouth. I am like the red bird on the maple branch calling out for my love, calling out for my beloved; your sweet sweet name.

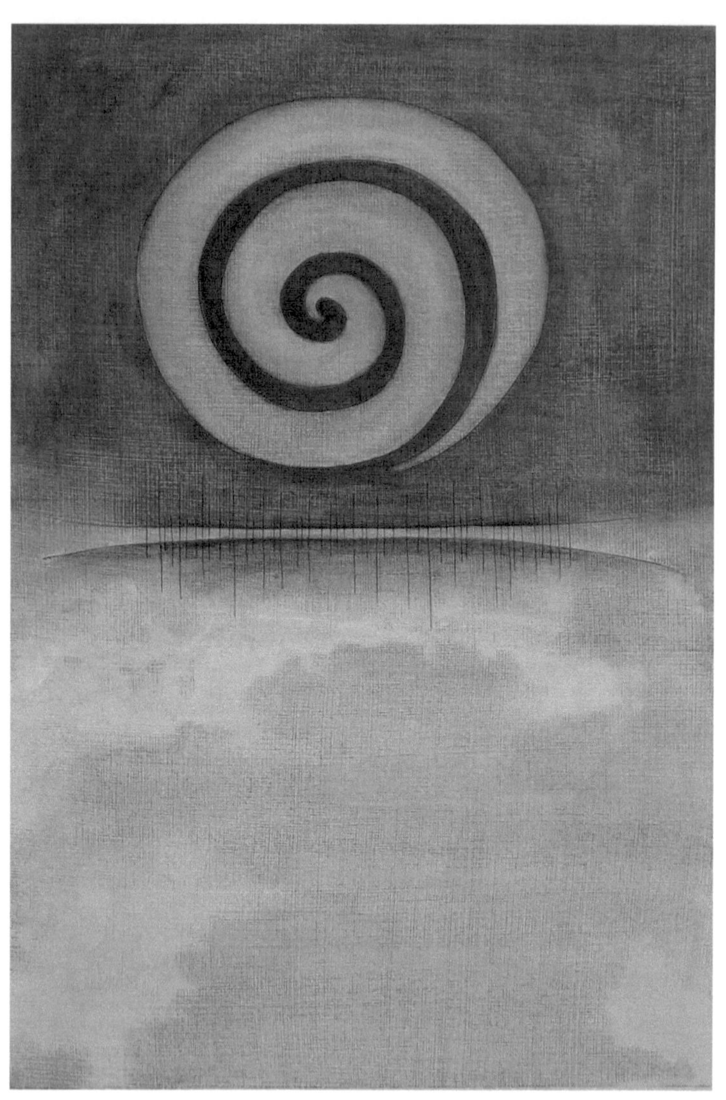

Post: From the Book of Remembrance (Pouring Rain)

•

I bring to you my broken body, like bread, broken in remembrance of you. I bring to you my empty heart to be made a chalice of. Like a tulip cupped to collect the healing waters of you. I am nothing but this agony and your tender intimacy. Nothing if I do not come to you wrecked, true. I say this but of course I want to come to you whole already, not in ruins but in glowing radiance. How hard to stand before you in my naked woundedness, to let you see me, let you love me, even here in the pouring rain.

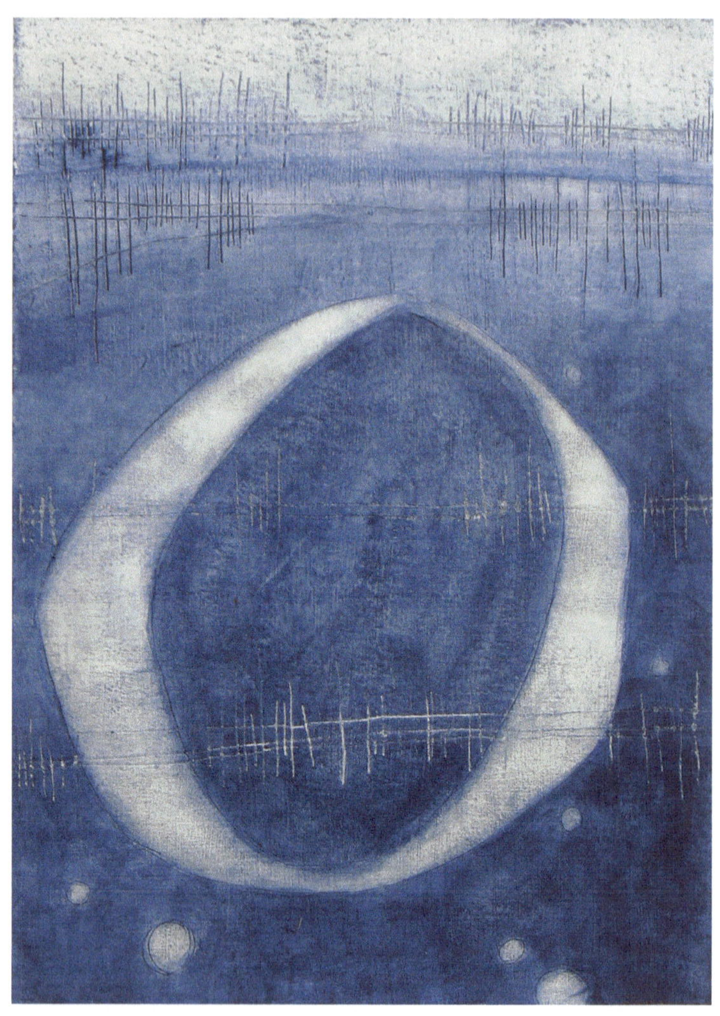

Post: From the Book of Remembrance (You and I)

•

Years went by, one after the other. Around Bristol Pond the fields were tilled, planted, offered up their plenty, then died back to ground. Above, the sky lit to the east then darkened as the sun plummeted west. And then one night you came in a dream and I recognized you, my beloved, my God. It is strange to think of the one hundred billion stars born each year. How big the universe. And you and I. You entered and I rose like flame to meet you, a consummation. Let me blaze like a thousand gases, let me disassemble cast myself into fever, into fusion like a resurrection. Like one of those stars formed of light and force. My fire, so utterly yours.

About the Poet / Artist

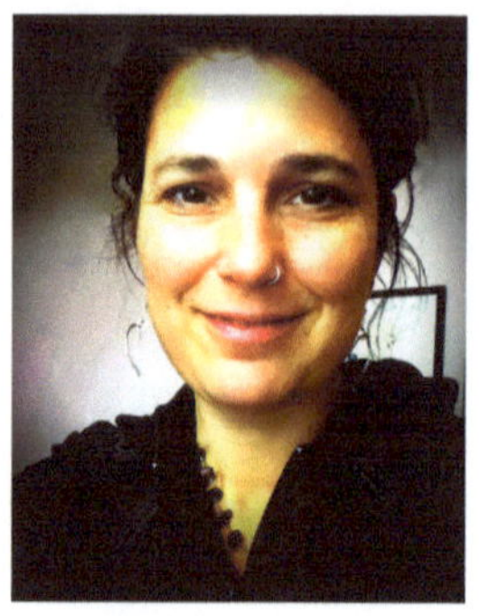

Karla Van Vliet studied visual art at Bennington College. She received her B.A. from Goddard College and her M.F.A. in Poetry from Vermont College of Fine Arts. She is the co-founder and editor of *deLuge*, a literary and arts journal. Her poems have appeared in such journals as *Poet Lore, Painted Bride Quarterly,* and *Tishman Review.* Van Vliet's book of poems entitled *The River From My Mouth* (North of Eden Press) was published in 2010. She is a Dreamwork analyst and administrator of the New England Young Writers' Conference at Bread Loaf, Middlebury College. Van Vliet lives in Bristol, Vermont.

www.ingramcontent.com/pod-product-compliance
Lightning Source LLC
LaVergne TN
LVHW052309100826
845147LV00006B/714

* 9 7 8 1 9 4 1 8 3 0 2 3 9 *